WEIRD, WACKY SCIENCE

Sandra Markle

Illustrated by Cecile Schoberle

Hyperion Paperbacks for Children
New York

Printed in the United States of America.

First Edition

1 3 5 7 9 10 8 6 4 2

The artwork for each picture is prepared using pen and ink.
This book is set in 14-point Adobe Garamond.
Designed by Arlene Goldberg.

Library of Congress Cataloging-in-Publication Data
Markle, Sandra.
Weird, wacky science / Sandra Markle — 1st ed.
p.   cm.
Summary: Presents facts revealing some of the strange and even weird aspects of
humans, animals, and general science while also suggesting experiments related
to this information.
ISBN: 0-7868-1089-0 (pbk.)—ISBN: 0-7868-2179-5 (lib. bdg.)
1. Science—Miscellanea—Juvenile literature. 2. Science—Experiments—Juvenile
literature. 3. Scientific recreations—Juvenile literature. 4. Body, Human—Juvenile
literature. 5. Animals—Juvenile literature. [1. Science—Miscellanea. 2. Science—
Experiments. 3. Scientific recreations. 4. Experiments. 5. Animals.] I. Title.
Q173.M312   1998
500—dc21   97-39344

CONTENTS

Would you like to be able to do some weird science magic? How would you like to make a water balloon that is stuck inside a bottle pop out easily? Would you like to find out a detective's secrets for making seemingly invisible fingerprints visible? How about learning how to use several sheets of newspaper to break a yardstick?

You can do all these things and more! All you'll need are materials you can find at home or that you can buy at a grocery store, gardening store, or hardware store. As you investigate, you'll discover some basic science concepts and use these to do even more exciting things. You'll also have plenty of chances to brainstorm and then experiment in order to test your ideas.

Here are steps you can work through to tackle a problem-solving situation:

1) Consider everything you already know about the problem. What did you learn by doing an earlier investigation? Is there anything you could look up at the library?

2) Brainstorm possible solutions. Give yourself fifteen minutes to write down every idea that comes into your head.

3) Analyze your list of possible solutions. Be critical as you consider reasons why your ideas might not work. Choose the idea you think has the best chance of success. Be sure to check with an adult that what you want to try is safe.

4) Test your solution. If you are setting up an experiment, be sure that everything is identical except the one thing you want to change. For example, in the first activity when you're testing to see if different-sized goblets produce different tones, the amount of water poured into the goblets and the way you stroke the rims should be identical. The goblets should also be side by side on the same surface. Only the *size* of the goblets should be different. Each goblet should also be tested at least three times

to be sure the results you get are what is likely to happen every time.

5) Always analyze the results of your test. Did your idea work? From what you discovered, is there anything else you could try that might work even better?

REMEMBER

*You will need to have an adult partner share some of these activities.

*Clean up the work area after you finish your activity.

*Recycle materials whenever possible.

*Have fun!

WEIRD,
WACKY
SCIENCE

YOUR REALLY STRANGE BODY

You probably think you really know your body since you live in it and see it every day. But did you know your fingerprints can play music? Or that you can trick your eyes into making you think you are looking through a hole in your hand? You may also be surprised to discover that some pretty creepy critters live on you. Here are some wacky facts and investigations to let you discover how strange your body really is.

PUT THE FINGER ON CRIME

What is it that criminals can't disguise about themselves even if they try? It's fingerprints. Gangster John Dillinger tried to burn his fingerprints off with acid, but the pattern was visible even through the scar tissue. In fact, for more than a hundred years, fingerprints found at the scene of a crime have been pointing out who's guilty. The first case where fingerprints were used to convict a criminal was in 1892 in Buenos Aires, Argentina. Francisca Rojas had claimed that a neighbor murdered her sons, and detective Juan Vucetich found bloody fingerprints on a door. But when these turned out to match Francisca's prints, she was arrested and convicted of murder. Juan Vucetich and Edward Henry, who went on to become the head of the famous crime-solving team at Scotland Yard, published details of two clarification systems for fingerprints. These became the foundation for modern fingerprinting science.

Fingerprints are left at the scene every time a criminal touches something—unless he or she is wearing gloves. Human skin gives off sweat and oil. So when a finger touches a surface, a little of this residue is left behind in the same pattern as the fingerprint's ridges. Look closely at one of your fingertips. Use a magnifying glass if you have one. The ridges of skin on your fingertip are designed to let you get a good grip on things, but the pattern of those ridges and whorls are uniquely your own. No two people have exactly the same fingerprints—not even identical twins. In fact, each of your ten fingers, and even each of your toes, has its own special pattern. Check it out for yourself.

To collect a set of fingerprints, rub a soft pencil back and forth on a piece of paper until you've

Loop

Whorl

Arch

made a dirty smudge. Rub one fingertip across this black spot several times. Next, press a piece of transparent tape on your dirty finger, peel it off, and stick it to a clean sheet of white paper. Now, you can take a really close look at your print. Scientists who study fingerprints report being able to identify as many as one hundred and fifty different characteristics in a single print. Most fingerprints fall into one of three main groups: arched, looped or whorled.

How forensic experts (scientists who collect clues about a crime) collect fingerprints depends on the surface being examined. Here are two methods you can try for yourself.

1) Dust For Prints

You'll need:
   drinking glass
   clean towel
   baby powder
   straw
   magnifying glass
   piece of black construction paper

Thoroughly wipe a drinking glass with a clean towel to erase any prints that may already be on it. If you have just washed your hands or your fingers feel dry, rub them across your forehead to collect some oil. Then pick up the glass, gripping it firmly. Now, after putting the glass down, sprinkle baby powder lightly over the glass and puff gently

through a straw to blow away any excess powder. You should see dusty fingerprints on the glass.

To collect the prints, place transparent tape over the dusty prints, peel the tape off, and stick it to a piece of black paper. Examine the prints with a magnifying class. How closely do they match your master set of prints?

2) Use Glue to Spot Prints

You'll need:
   plastic cup
   clean towel
   Super Glue®
   quart-size, self-sealing plastic bag
   2 pairs of rubber gloves
   magnifying glass
   2 pairs of safety goggles

Some surfaces, such as metal and plastic, don't readily collect dust to reveal prints. However, Super Glue makes it possible to collect prints even on these materials. To see how this works, have an adult partner help you try this test. First, wipe a plastic cup with a clean towel to erase any previous fingerprints. Once again, rub your forehead to increase the oil on your fingers and then pick up the cup, gripping it with your fingers.

Next, go outdoors to be sure there is plenty of fresh air. You should both put on goggles just to be safe. Have your adult partner put on rubber work gloves and drip a dozen drops of Super Glue into one corner of the plastic bag. Avoid breath-

ing the fumes or touching the glue. Put on rubber gloves yourself, place the cup inside the bag, and seal it. Set the bag on the ground and leave it for about three hours. Then, wearing gloves, remove the cup from the bag and examine it with a magnifying glass. You'll be able to see a faint but distinct fingerprint. According to forensic scientist Al Pryor of the Georgia State Crime Lab, this fingerprint is actually the result of a special chemical called *cyanoacrylate ester* in the glue's fumes. It's this chemical that produces a chalky powder outlining the prints. When you're finished, put the cup back into the bag and dispose of it with your family's trash.

Forensic scientists use other special techniques to reveal fingerprints on hard-to-test surfaces. After using special chemical dusts, laser light can reveal very faint fingerprints—sometimes even on cloth or skin. According to Eric Maddox, forensic technician with the Atlanta Police Department in Georgia, a chemical called *ninhydrin* makes it possible to reveal otherwise hard-to-see prints on paper. The paper that is thought to have fingerprints on it is dipped in a solution containing ninhydrin and agitated like clothes in a washing machine. This ensures that the paper will thoroughly absorb the chemical. Then the paper is removed from the solution, placed under a towel, and pressed with a steam iron. The ninhydrin reacts with any traces of oil or sweat left behind when fingers touched the paper. Steam causes the chemical to turn purple, revealing the fingerprints.

How do the police know from the fingerprints who the criminal is? They compare the prints found at the scene of the crime with those of the suspects or from fingerprints kept on file. You may want to start a file of fingerprints by collecting those of your friends and family. A file will let you compare fingerprints to see how they are alike and how they are different. Studies have shown that despite individual differences, the greatest number of people have fingerprints with a whorled pattern.

In addition to fingerprints and toe prints, each person's palm print and footprint is also unique. So these prints can also be used to check someone's identity if necessary.

CAN YOUR FINGERPRINTS CREATE MUSIC?

It's weird! It's wacky! It's possible! The ridges that form your fingerprints can let you produce sounds—actual musical tones. Try this to create music yourself. Then read on to find out what happens to produce the sounds you hear.

You'll need:
   **a good crystal goblet
   (get an adult's permission)
   a cup of water**

The goblet must be good crystal because then the entire rim can be counted on to be a consistent thickness. Inexpensive glasses tend to be of an uneven thickness. This is true even if you can't easily detect the difference.

To produce a sound, first dip your index fingertip into the cup of water. Then rub your wet finger around the rim of the goblet. Keep circling the rim even when your fingertip starts to stick a little as it slides. You should hear a bell-like tone.

The ridges that form your fingerprint stick to the glass and then suddenly slip forward, usually so quickly that you aren't aware of the jump. This little jerk, though, is enough to make the glass vibrate. When the glass vibrates, air molecules vibrate. These vibrations are detected by your ears. Messages are transmitted to the brain, and when your brain interprets them you hear the sound loud and clear. Again, it is important that you try this with good crystal because the irregularities along the rim of a cheap glass can disrupt the pattern. This will prevent vibrations from building up and thus stop the music.

The tone produced by the glass will seem to get louder if you keep on rubbing the rim. This is the same effect created when the string of a musical instrument is plucked more than once. The effect is called *resonance*. Resonance means that matching vibrations are produced over and over, reinforcing one another and increasing the volume.

Do different goblets produce different sounds? Get your adult partner's permission to test several different goblets and then let your fingers be musical.

WHO IS LIVING ON YOU?

You may think your body is yours alone. Guess again. You're practically a walking apartment house. Every year your body sheds millions of dead skin cells—as much as 18 kilograms (40 pounds) of dead skin by the age of seventy. The disgusting part is that all this dead skin is a feast for mites—millions of tiny animals that live on your body. This is generally a peaceful arrangement, except for people who are allergic to mites, which sometimes float away with dust in the air and can be inhaled

Of course, mites aren't the only critters living on your body. In addition to the mites, about every 2.5 centimeter square (one square inch) of healthy clean skin contains 5 million tiny living things called *microbes*. Every mouthful of spit is home to at least 10 million bacteria. You get rid of as many as 100 billion microbes every time your bowels move, but these are quickly replaced. The good news is that being a host to mites, bacteria, and microbes is all perfectly normal—it is even healthy.

LOOK THROUGH A HOLE IN YOUR HAND!

Does that sound too weird to be possible? You can do it once you know the science that make this seemingly magical trick work. All you need is a sheet of paper rolled and taped to form a tube.

Hold the tube up to your left eye and focus on looking through it. Now, hold your right hand up with your fingers together and the palm side

HERE'S WHAT YOU'LL SEE

toward your face. Position your right hand so it's about 12 centimeters (between 4 and 5 inches) from your right eye. Focus on looking through the tube, and move your hand slightly toward and away from your face. What you see of your hand should appear to have a hole sliced out of it where the tube passes through.

This happens because each of your eyes receives a separate set of light images and each sends a separate set of messages to your brain. The brain has developed the ability to combine these images so that what you "see" is actually what your brain interprets from these dual signals. Here's another test to let you see that the image detected by each of your eyes is slightly different. Roll a scarf and tie it around your head to create a patch that covers just one eye. Have your adult partner stand 2 meters (between 6 and 7 feet) away and toss you paper wadded into a ball.

Can you catch the paper wad? Repeat this test four more times. Then try it again without the eye patch and using both eyes.

You probably caught the ball more often and more easily when you were using both eyes. By seeing the ball with two eyes, you saw it from two slightly different angles. Your brain has learned to use this information to judge distance, and this information helps you time the act of reaching out to catch the wad of paper.

CAN YOU KEEP FROM YAWNING?

You probably can't—even if you try. Studies show that even reading about yawning is likely to start the process. So why do you yawn?

According to a report by Dr. Francisco Gonzalez-Lima, Professor of Neuroscience and Psychology at the University of Texas in Austin, yawning is a reflex action designed to help bring the body back to normal, just as a cough is a reflex action designed to get rid of anything irritating that enters your windpipe, and a sneeze is a reflex

to discharge anything irritating that gets into the nasal air passages. A yawn is a reflex that happens when your body's nerve cells assess that there is too much carbon dioxide in the blood. Carbon dioxide is the waste gas that is produced when oxygen and food nutrients combine to produce energy—the energy your body needs to be active and to grow.

A yawn causes the muscles in your mouth and throat to contract. This forces your mouth to open wide, allowing you to take in a large amount of air with a fresh supply of oxygen. Breathing out at the end of a yawn expels air containing the excess carbon dioxide.

Are yawns contagious? You may have noticed that if you see someone yawn you can't seem to help yawning yourself. Some people believe that yawning is a learned response. Over the years humans have learned to yawn when we see others yawn. In time, the link has become so strong that just seeing or thinking about yawning is enough to trigger that response. Try yawning on purpose the next time you are with your family or in a group. Then observe how many people yawn after you.

According to Lynn Bry, an M.D./Ph.D. student in molecular biology at Washington University in St. Louis, yawning is also something we do when we're tired but nobody is sure why. Perhaps taking a deep breath and the intake of oxygen is your body's way of refreshing itself. If you also stretch while yawning, the moving muscles help blood circulate the fresh oxygen supply around the body. In the meantime, getting a good gulp of oxygen-rich air will refresh your body, and yawning can also help stretch your facial muscles.

How many times did you yawn while reading these pages?

CAN YOU KEEP FROM BLINKING?

Bet you can't. Closing your eyes quickly is a reflex action. At the slightest hint of an intrusion, your eyelid flaps down to shield your eye.

Did you know that it's impossible to keep your eyes open when you sneeze? That's because when you sneeze, you spray germs that could get into your eyes and infect them. Of course, you don't just blink when your eyes are threatened. Blinking

Achoo!

Bless you.

23

also helps wash the surface of your eyes with tears. This not only helps clear away bits of dust; tears also contain a substance called *lysozyme,* which kills germs. Watch somebody for one minute to count the number of blinks. On the average, people blink twenty-five times a minute. How many blinks an hour is that?

TRICK YOUR TASTE BUDS

Can you make your taste buds believe you're eating apple pie when you're not? This may sound weird, but it's just the kind of trick artificial flavorings pull on your taste buds all the time. Follow the directions below to make a fake apple pie—one that doesn't contain a single apple. Then take a bite to see if your taste buds can be fooled even when you know the truth. Then read on to learn more about the weird science of artificial flavors.

You'll need:
  9-inch pie plate
  saucepan
  oven mitts
  mixing bowl, fork
  36 Ritz crackers
  rolling pin
  cooling rack
  measuring cup
  measuring spoons
  2 cups granulated sugar
  2 teaspoons cream of tartar

2 tablespoons lemon juice
2 tablespoons margarine
1/2 teaspoon cinnamon
waxed paper
1 3/4 cups flour
1 teaspoon salt
1/2 cup vegetable oil

You'll be using the stove so work with an adult partner and follow the directions carefully to stay safe.

First, prepare the crust. Pour the flour into the mixing bowl and add the salt and oil. Blend with the fork until crumbly. Sprinkle three tablespoons

of cold water over the dough. Press the dough into a ball with your hands. Divide the dough in half. Spread out two 35-centimeter (about 14 inches)-long sheets of waxed paper. Put a fourth teaspoon of flour between the sheets and rub back and forth to coat. Place half of the dough between the two waxed paper sheets. Roll until the pastry is larger than the pie pan. Peel off the top paper and turn the pie pan upside down over the pastry. Turn over and press the pastry against the sides of the pan. Roll out the second half of the dough so it's ready to top the pie.

Next, coarsely crumble thirty-six Ritz crackers, spreading them on top of the pastry in the pie pan.

Pour two cups of water into a saucepan. Add the sugar and cream of tartar. Stir and bring to a boil over high heat. Reduce the heat setting and simmer for fifteen minutes or until the sugar sauce has thickened. Have your adult partner use oven mitts to transfer the saucepan to the cooling rack. Add the lemon juice and let the sugar sauce cool.

Pour the sauce over the crackers. Dot with margarine and sprinkle on the cinnamon. Top with the remaining crust. Press the edges together to seal and then prick the top crust with the fork so steam can escape. Bake at 425°F (218.33°C) for thirty minutes.

Have your adult partner use oven mitts to transfer the pie pan to the cooling rack. Let cool completely. Enjoy!

Wondering how crackers can taste like apple pie? Alice Schedlbauer, nutritionist from Nabisco, the makers of Ritz crackers, explained that the ingredients trick your senses. The crackers puff up from the liquid, providing the texture of baked apple. The lemon juice, sugary syrup, and cinnamon combine to simulate the sweet-tart, spicy taste of apple pie. The recipe for this fake apple pie originated during the Depression when crackers were a lot cheaper than apples.

Scientists have discovered other food flavors can be simulated in laboratories. This is possible because foods contain special chemicals that give them their specific taste. For example, garlic contains the naturally occurring chemical *allyl isothiocyanate*. It's this chemical that gives garlic its distinctive flavor and also gives people garlic breath. This chemical, though, can be produced synthetically so it isn't necessary to grow and crush garlic to obtain this flavoring for food. Likewise, *ethyl caproate* is used to imitate fruit flavors, especially pineapple.

C11-Undeyl aldehyde provides an orange flavor, and *ethyl phenylacetate* adds the taste of honey to many foods.

Many times, artificial flavorings are preferred to the real flavoring material for three reasons: 1) they're cheaper to produce; 2) the quality can be counted on to be consistent; 3) they're available year-round while the real thing is often seasonal.

CAN A POTATO TASTE LIKE AN APPLE?

Weird as this sounds, it's possible for a potato and an apple to taste the same. And this time there are no artificial flavorings. The trick works because part of tasting foods is smelling them. To prove the importance of smell in tasting, cut a potato and an apple into identical small cubes. Put on a blindfold and pinch your nose closed. Stick out your tongue and have an adult partner put either a piece of apple or a piece of potato into your mouth.

Close your mouth but don't chew because you might get clues from the food's texture. Can you identify the food by the flavor alone? When you feel like you need a breath, unpinch your nose, but don't chew. As soon as you become aware of the food's smell, you'll probably be able to identify it. Now you know why foods seem to be less flavorful and sometimes even taste weird when your nose is stopped up from a cold or allergies.

Here's something else weird about taste. Most animals have taste sensors in their mouths the way you do. A butterfly, though, has special taste sensors on its feet. And fish have taste sensors over

Yum Yum!

various parts of their body. Bony fish have taste sensors inside their mouth with taste buds on the walls of their mouth and the tongue. Other types of fish have taste buds on the outer surface of their heads and lips and at the tips of their fins. A few species of fish have whiskerlike parts which contain special structures sensitive to taste. These external taste buds enable the fish to evaluate food before they eat it.

CAN YOU HOLD YOUR HAND STILL?

Do you believe you can hold your hand perfectly still? Then try this activity to find out why that's impossible.

You'll need:
   a ruler
   a paper clip

Have an adult partner bend the paper clip into a V shape. Next, hold the ruler in one hand so the narrow edge is on top. Have your adult partner place the v-clip over the ruler about 5 centimeters (2 inches) from the end away from your body. Now, hold your arm outstretched over a table so the points of the clip just touch the surface. Focus on keeping the ruler steady.

Surprise! It's impossible to totally eliminate movement, and the amount of motion may even startle you. The movement is caused by tiny contractions of the muscles that are pulling on the bones in your arm to hold them in this out-stretched position. To be able to move, your

muscles work in pairs, pulling on bones. Although slight, these contractions are enough to jiggle the clip and may even wiggle it right off the end of the ruler. Oxygen and muscle *glycogen*—formed from blood sugar called glucose—is needed to power the contractions. When the contractions use up the oxygen supply, a waste chemical called *lactic acid* is produced. The more lactic acid builds up the slower the muscle's response time becomes. Your arm will probably begin to ache. The muscle contractions keeping the bones of your arm in this outstretched position will become farther apart so the contraction motion will be more noticeable. You may even feel as if your arm is jerking. Finally, your muscles will be exhausted and they will stop contracting and your arm will ache painfully. Then you'll have to let the muscles rest. The blood continues to bring a supply of oxygen to the muscles and this oxidizes the lactic acid, transforming it to *pyruvic acid* which is resynthesized into muscle glycogen. Once this process takes place, the muscles are ready to contract again.

Extra-Weird Challenge:

The human body has more than six hundred muscles, which contract to move different parts of the body. There are even lots of small muscles that let you create different facial expressions—some of them pretty weird-looking. Check out what you can accomplish for yourself by watching in a mirror. You'll probably think of other things to try with your facial muscles, but here are a few to get you started: lift your eyebrows, lift just one eyebrow, wrinkle your forehead, wiggle your ears, make your nostrils pinch shut (without touching them), make your nostrils flare open, pull your upper lip over your lower lip, curl your lips back, smile with just half of your mouth, and wink just one eye. Combine some of these facial moves to put on the weirdest expression you can manage.

If you want to conserve your muscles, smile. It only takes seventeen muscles to smile, but it requires the action of forty-three muscles to frown. Wondering why a frown requires so much muscles power? For starters, the *frontalis* and *corrugatorsupercilii* furrow your brow, the *nasalis* widens the nostrils, the *orbicularis oculi* narrows the eyes, the *platysma* and *depressors* pull the corners of the lips down and sideways, and

the *mentalis* puckers the chin. Look at yourself in the mirror as you smile and then frown. How many different, complex changes do you see happening to your expression?

WEIRD ANIMALS

You may have seen some pretty unusual animals at the zoo, but wait until you learn about *this* weird animal behavior. Did you know some fish actually spend the night wrapped in slime? Can you guess why they do this? You may also be surprised to learn what happens to a walrus in the sunshine or what a flamingo needs to eat to stay pink. The following facts will let you explore how amazing—and weird—some animals can be.

SOME FISH SPEND THE NIGHT IN A SLIMY SACK

This may sound disgustingly weird, but it's true. As night falls, the coral reef becomes a dark, spooky forest. Many of the colorful fish that have been active all day become quiet and find places to hide from nighttime hunters. Some parrotfish do even more to protect themselves. They secrete a thick gelatinlike mucus until they are com-pletely encased in a slimy sack. The kinds of parrotfish that do these slippery tricks include the striped parrotfish *(Scarus taeniopterus)* found in the West Indies, the rainbow parrotfish *(Scarus guacamaia)* found in the Atlantic from Florida to Argentina, and another striped parrotfish *(Scarus croicensis)* found from Massachusetts to the Gulf of Mexico and Brazil.

Although scientists aren't certain why the parrotfish construct a slimy sack, they suspect it's a smell mask. Moray eels and other nighttime predators on the reef have a keen sense of smell that helps them locate their prey. Wrapped in a slimy sack, the parrotfish's body odors are sealed inside with the fish. The one drawback is that it

takes time for the fish to form the sack—as long as thirty minutes. In the morning when natural light triggers the parrotfish to escape the slime, it sometimes struggles almost as long to break free.

CAN YOU BALANCE LIKE A BIRD?

The next time you're at the zoo, check out one of the long-legged birds, such as the flamingo. You'll discover that these birds often rest standing on just one leg. Take a close look at how they're holding their body. Like you, the bird has its weight balanced over its center of gravity. The bird's pose may look weird, but standing on just one leg actually makes it harder for a gust of wind to knock the bird off balance.

So how long could you stand on one leg? When you walk or run or jump, you are actually constantly shifting your weight from side to side to keep balanced. Try standing on just one leg. Have someone time you to see how long you can hold your flamingolike pose before you have to shift your weight.

Would leaning against a wall make it easier or harder to stand on one leg? Try it and find out. Stand with your left shoulder and hip pressed firmly against a wall. Now, lift your right leg. Surprise! You probably will not be able to lift your leg. If you did, you probably lowered your right leg immediately or shifted your weight away from the wall to stay balanced.

In case you're wondering why flamingos don't just lie down to rest, it's to stay safe. If an enemy sneaks up on a flamingo, the bird can take off faster if it's standing up.

DO PINK FLAMINGOS HAVE TO EAT TO STAY PINK?

It's strange, but true. Pink flamingos need a special chemical, *canthaxanthin,* in their diet to stay pink. Without this chemical the birds plumage fades dramatically. In the wild, the birds are able to eat plenty of live shrimp that contain *beta-carotene,* a natural source of canthaxanthin. Kelsey Riff, Assistant Librarian at Zoo Atlanta, in Georgia, reports that at Zoo Atlanta flamingos have to receive *roxanthin red,* a special dietary supplement that supplies enough canthaxanthin to keep the birds "in the pink" because the shrimp fed to flamingoes in a zoo is ground-up, thus losing its special chemical.

THESE ANIMALS ARE WACKY— MAYBE

1) Cowbirds are such hard-working birds they often help feed the young of other kinds of birds. True or False.

2) There is one kind of fish that catches insects in trees. True or False.

3) Sometimes large groups of ratlike animals, called lemmings, swim into the ocean in an attempt to find a new home. True or False.

4) A walrus's brown skin turns pink while it's lying on a rock in the sun, but it isn't getting sunburned. True or False.

5) Rabbits can blink their noses. True or False.

SOLUTIONS:

1) FALSE. The truth is that these lazy birds don't even incubate their eggs, let alone feed the growing babies. Instead, the cowbird lays its eggs in the nest of another bird. The young cowbird is often larger and grows faster than its foster parent's real babies. So the cowbird may even push the other chicks out of the nest.

2) **TRUE.** The Australian walking fish usually swims in water like a normal fish, but it sometimes crawls out of the water—even into the lowest branches on a tree. This fish has fins bent in such a way that it can walk on them. While most fish would die out of water, the Australian walking fish is capable of spending several hours at a time on land.

3) **TRUE.** Large numbers of lemmings swim out into the ocean, but they don't survive the trip. Lemmings usually live in colonies in the far north. But when the colony grows so big that food becomes scarce, hundreds—even thousands—of lemmings set off on a journey that may last a year or two. Finally, the swarm

of lemmings reaches the sea and plunges into the water. No one knows why they swim until they drown. Those that remained behind keep

on reproducing. The lemming population continues to grow—until food becomes scarce once again.

4) **TRUE.** The walrus's skin changes color as a result of a change in its blood flow. It often swims in icy-cold water, but the walrus maintains a steady, warm internal body tempera-

ture. Its blood carries heat energy that is directed away from the outer skin and thick layers of blubber. While lying in the sun, the process is reversed and blood flows close to the surface where excess heat can be released. This increased surface blood flow makes the walruss' skin appear pink.

5) **TRUE.** Tiny flaps of skin cover a rabbit's nostrils for a split second—a nose blink. Wondering why? Have you ever noticed how strongly you can smell food cooking when you first

come into the house from outdoors? After a while, though, the scent seems to get weaker. What's really happening is that your nose stops sending smell signals to your brain. Rabbits need their noses to stay alert to smell dangerous predators. Nose blinks let them do that.

Do a Beaver's Teeth Ever Stop Growing?

A beaver's front teeth are large and designed for the special job of gnawing wood to chop down trees. The teeth have a tough outer layer and a soft inner layer, giving them a chisellike edge that is actually sharpened by rubbing and gnashing. A beaver's teeth don't wear out either. Unlike *your* teeth, a beaver's teeth continue to grow as fast as they are worn down.

The beaver's lips are able to close around and

behind these big front teeth, which stick out in front of the lips, thus blocking water from entering its mouth. This lets the beaver gnaw wood under water without choking. Beavers eat leaves and ferns and algae in the spring and summer, but during the fall and winter they mainly eat woody stems. Storing this woody material underwater is like putting the food in the refrigerator. Being cold and wet maintains the wood's nutritional value. Special microbes in the beaver's intestine help it digest this tough plant meal.

WACKY SCIENCE MAGIC

You probably think of science as practical. It helps people explore the world and solve problems. Science does that, but sometimes it can produce results that appear magical. For example, you can use a single sheet of newspaper to help you break a yardstick. You can also make your breath appear to pass through a plastic bottle, or make a water-filled balloon pop into a bottle by itself. Here are some wacky science investigations that will surprise you.

MAKE A BALLOON POP INTO A JAR

It's weird! It's amazing! You can do it once you know the science that makes it happen. Then when the balloon appears stuck inside the bottle, you can make it pop out once again. Just follow these steps to learn how to perform this wacky science magic.

You'll need to burn a piece of paper so work with an adult partner outdoors and follow the steps carefully to stay safe.

You'll need:
   a round rubber balloon
   a glass quart jar
   a piece of notebook paper
   scissors
   a long fireplace match
   2 tablespoons vegetable oil
   paper towel
   2 pairs of safety goggles
   straw

Before you go outdoors, hold the mouth of the balloon under the faucet to fill the balloon with water. Add water until the balloon is just fat enough to sit on the quart jar without slipping through the opening. Have your adult partner tie a knot in the neck of the water balloon to seal it. Pour the vegetable oil onto the paper towel and take everything outdoors to a sidewalk.

Cut the paper in half width-wise. Accordion-fold half of the paper and drop it into the quart jar. Rub half the balloon with the oily paper towel. Have your adult partner use the match to light the paper inside the jar and immediately set the water balloon—oiled side down—on the mouth of the jar.

The bottom of the balloon will sink into the

jar until—POP, it drops into the jar. This weird, magical event actually happens because the burning paper used up the oxygen from the air inside the jar. Hot air expands and some of this air squeezed out past the balloon. In fact, you may have noticed that the water balloon bobbled a bit before it plopped into the jar. Once the paper has burned up, the air that remains quickly cools and contracts so it takes up less space. The water balloon is a plug, letting no new air into the jar. So the air pressure outside the jar is greater than the air pressure inside the jar, and the water balloon is pushed in.

If this doesn't happen, dump the ashes out of the jar, make a slightly smaller water balloon, and try again. Once it does work, you're ready

to perform a second weird stunt with a little help from science—getting the water balloon out of the jar. Hold the jar tipped so the water balloon is at the opening, plugging it. Squeeze the straw into the jar past the balloon and blow into the jar three times. Pull the straw out and turn the jar straight upside down. This time the air inside the jar should force the water balloon out.

MAKE PAPER PUT ON THE PRESSURE

Can something as thin as newspaper be enough to anchor a yardstick on a table? It can when you know a science secret. Just follow the directions to do something that looks a lot like magic.

You will be breaking the wood, so work with an adult partner and be sure to wear safety goggles.

You'll need:
> 3 two-page spreads of newspaper
> yardstick
> > (inexpensive kind available at
> > hardware stores)
> table with a flat surface
> 2 pairs of safety goggles

You and your adult partner should both wear safety goggles just to be extra safe when performing this science magic stunt. Be sure your table is steady and that it is away from anything that could break.

Lay the yardstick on the table so that about 10

centimeters (4 inches) sticks out over the edge.
Cover the part of the yardstick that is on the table
with the sheets of newspaper, stacked one on top
of the other. Smooth the newspaper flat.

Next, stand beside the table, put on your
safety goggles, and hit the part of the yardstick
that is sticking out with your fist. Be sure to hit it
hard and fast, like a karate chop. Surprise! That
piece of yardstick should break off.

Wondering why the yardstick did not just flip

up? The answer is that the newspaper anchored the end of the yardstick. How could the newspaper be that heavy—heavy enough to hold down the yardstick?

The newspaper itself is not that heavy. Because the paper had a lot of surface area, there was a lot of air pressing down. We are used to air around us, pushing down, pressing up, and pushing in on all sides. So we don't realize that air, in fact, has weight. In this case, it had enough weight to anchor the yardstick.

BLOW THROUGH THE BOTTLE

Can you blow through a bottle? You can make it *look* like you can when you know a science secret about air.

A stream of air that strikes straight onto a curved surface will split into separate parts and slide in two directions around that circular surface. Then the air stream will reunite and continue in a straight path. Now you can use this to do something that looks like magic.

You'll need:
   a quart jar
   a strip of typing paper 5 x 1 inches
      (about 12 x 2.5 centimeters)
   tape
   table with flat top
      (you'll be putting tape on the top, so be sure
      you have an adult's permission to use
      the table)

To see the effect, you will need to have the table away from any drafts. Set the quart jar on the table about 7 centimeters (3 inches) from the edge. Fold up the end of the paper strip, forming a flap. Tape the flap to the table about 10 centimeters (4 inches) from the jar and directly behind it. Fold up the paper so it is standing straight up.

To perform this stunt, you will need to sit or kneel so that you are directly in front of the jar and at the same level as the paper strip. Now, blow hard. Take a breath and blow again. You should be able to see the paper fluttering from your breath. It looks like you are blowing through the jar, but you know the truth. You are simply getting a little help from science.

60

Once you have this stunt down pat, you may want to try a variation—blowing out a candle. Just remember the rule. You have to blow a stream of air at the same level as the candle's flame. You will also have to blow hard. It takes a stronger puff of air to blow out a candle flame than to make the paper flutter. But have your adult partner help you set this stunt up, and give it a try.

MAKE A WEIRD GEEHAW THINGAMAJIG

This wild and wacky toy appears to have some magical powers of its own, but once again it's science acting like magic. This toy may have entertained your grandparents or even your great-grandparents. It's been fun for over a century.

You'll need:
  2 straight sticks or wooden dowels,
      about 1 centimeter (1/2 inch) thick and
      18 centimeters (7 inches) long
  pliers
  a saw or file
  a hammer
  a ruler
  a nail
  a popsicle stick (cut in half width-wise)

Mark the center of the flat wood strip. Have your adult partner hammer the nail through this mark halfway into the center of one end of the stick. Using the pliers, wiggle the nail until the wooden strip can spin freely like a propeller.

Next, measure about 5 centimeters (2 inches) from the nail and make a mark on the top of the stick. Measure about 1 centimeter (half inch) from this mark and make a second mark. Make nine more marks at this same distance apart on the top of the stick. Have your adult partner use the saw or file to cut notches at an angle, slanting toward the nail. Each notch should extend about a quarter of the way through the stick.

Now, you're ready to see this weird toy in action. You're going to rub the smooth stick vigorously

over the notches. So hold the notched stick in one hand-propeller aimed away from you—and briskly rub the smooth stick back and forth. You'll hear a noise as the propeller starts turning. The sound is created by the vibrations of the stick hitting the notches.

The propeller turns because rubbing the stick over the notches sets up vibrations. If you've ever looked at a tree stump and seen the growth rings, you know that this natural pattern in the wood tends to be asymmetrical rather than perfectly round. So as the vibrations pass through the notched stick, they tend to move more toward one side of the stick than the other. This sets up a motion that starts the propeller moving. Repeatedly stroking the stick makes the vibrations overlap, increasing the intensity—enough to make the propeller spin.

Here's one more trick you should be able to manage with a little practice. While the geehaw thingamajig's propeller is spinning, pull on the notched stick slightly with your thumb or fingers. If this doesn't change the direction the propeller is turning, gently push the notched stick away instead. The circular motion created by the vibrations will tend to be either clockwise or counter-clockwise. Pulling or pushing the stick will change the direction of that motion and that should make the propeller spin in the opposite direction.

MAKE IT KEEP SWINGING

Imagine being able to set a pendulum swinging without even touching it. Or making two pendulums pass energy back and forth so first one swings, then the other, and so forth. Sound weird? It looks like magic, but it works because of science. You have to see it to believe it.

You'll need:
   string
   scissors
   paper tape (also called masking tape)
   a table (you'll be putting tape on the top
      so be sure you have an adult's permission
      to use the table)
   two identical metal washers
   ruler
   medium-sized rubber band

Cut two pieces of string about 37 centimeters (15 inches) long. Tie one washer to one end of each string. Suspend one string from the side of the table so the metal washer is able to swing without hitting the table leg. What

you've just created is called a *pendulum*.

Secure the string by taping it to the tabletop. Measure over 10 centimeters (4 inches) and suspend the second string beside the first. Make it hang at exactly the same level, be sure the metal washer is able to swing freely, and anchor the string in place. Next, slide the rubber band up over the washers until it's about 12 centimeters (5 inches) from the edge of the tabletop. If the rubber band doesn't stay in place when you let go, you'll need to use a smaller rubber band. To start

the action, sit or stand in front of the paired pendulums. Hold just one of the two washers, pull it toward you, and let go.

Long ago in Italy, a young man named Galileo Galilei watched a lantern swinging on a long chain just the way the washer is swinging on the string. Galileo rigged his own suspended weight, which he called a pendulum, in order to try some experiments. Just like Galileo, you'll discover that as the first pendulum swings, it passes on the energy of this motion to the second pendulum. Eventually, the first pendulum has so little energy left that it swings more slowly and may even stop. Meanwhile, the second pendulum has built up enough energy to start it swinging. Gradually, the second pendulum will pass the energy of its swinging motion back to the first pendulum. Then the second pendulum will slow to near stopping and the first pendulum will begin to swing again.

Time how long the pendulums keep swinging. And count how many times the energy is conducted or passed from the first pendulum to the second one. Each time, of course, a little of the energy is also conducted away through the string to the table as vibrations and is lost. So, finally, there isn't enough energy left to propel either pendulum forward and backward. Which pendulum is the last to swing?

Now, go on a pendulum hunt. You'll probably be surprised how many places you can find

pendulums once you know what you're looking for—a suspended weight that can swing freely. You'll probably find lots more, but here are a few to get you started: the pendulum on a grandfather clock, a church bell, a wrecking ball, a yo-yo suspended from its string, dangling earring, locket on a chain, soap on a rope, pull chain on light—all sorts of pendulums exist.